one-man band

I make music with my mouth, hands and feet.

Music has got a beat.

One   two   three   four!

beat

drum

click

I make a beat with my hands
and my feet.

click

click

The big beat is on three.

Music has got a tune.

A tune has got notes.
Here are eight notes.

I make a tune with my mouth.

recorder

guitar

8

Some tunes are happy.

violin

Some tunes are sad.

pop music

Do you like pop music?

I make music with things from my house.

Activities

Before You Read

1 Match. Now find the pictures in the book.

> violin   guitar   drum   recorder   piano

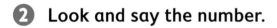

After You Read

1 Read and match.

a Some tunes are sad.
b Music has got notes.
c We play pop music.
d I make the beat.

2 Look and say the number.

a I make music with my hands.
b I make music with my mouth.
c I make music with my mouth and hands.

Pearson Education Limited
Edinburgh Gate, Harlow,
Essex CM20 2JE, England
and Associated Companies throughout the world.

ISBN: 978-1-4082-8821-4

This edition first published by Pearson Education Ltd 2013
9 10 8
Text copyright © Pearson Education Ltd 2013

The moral rights of the author have been asserted
in accordance with the Copyright Designs and Patents Act 1988

Set in 19/23pt OT Fiendstar
Printed in China
SWTC/08

Acknowledgements
The publisher would like to thank the following for their kind permission to reproduce their photographs:
(Key: b-bottom; c-centre; l-left; r-right; t-top)

Alamy Images: Daniel Dempster Photography 12, Larry Lilac 1, Laura Johansen 14 (boy); **DK Images:** Dave King 14tr, 14bc, Susanna Price 14br; **Fotolia.com:** Claus Aagaard 15 (b), IrisArt 15 (c), jeancliclac 4, Joss 15/1 (drummer), Kalim 6b, Pavel Losevsky 10-11, 13, 15/4 (band); **FotoLibra:** Anthony Free 7r, Ilex Press 7l; **PhotoDisc:** C Squared Studios. Tony Gable 15 (e); **Press Association Images:** Andre Penner / AP 9t, Mark Allan / AP 8t, Vit Simanek / Czech News Agency 6t; **Shutterstock.com:** artjazz 3, Hasan Shaheed 2, 15 (a), Jules Studio 15/1 (recorder), Monkey Business Images 15/2 (piano), Noam Armonn 5, Sandra van der Steen 15 (d), Yurchyks 15/3 (singing); **SuperStock:** Corbis 8b, moodboard 9b
Cover images: *Front*: **Alamy Images**: GoGo Images Corporation

All other images © Pearson Education

In some instances we have been unable to trace the owners of copyright material,
and we would appreciate any information that would enable us to do so.

Illustrations: Marek Jagucki

All rights reserved; no part of this publication may be reproduced, stored in a retrieval system,
or transmitted in any form or by any means, electronic, mechanical, photocopying,
recording or otherwise, without the prior written permission of the Publishers.

For a complete list of the titles available in the Pearson English Kids Readers series, please go to
www.pearsonenglishkidsreaders.com. Alternatively, write to your local Pearson Education office or to
Pearson English Readers Marketing Department, Pearson Education, Edinburgh Gate, Harlow, Essex CM202JE, England.